Sunny and Moonshine

illustrated by Joel Nakamura

written by Shirleyann Costigan

HAMPTON-BROWN

The Solar System

The Earth

The Earth is a planet. There are nine planets in our Solar System.

The Sun

The Sun is a star. There are billions of stars in the Universe.

Orbiting Planets

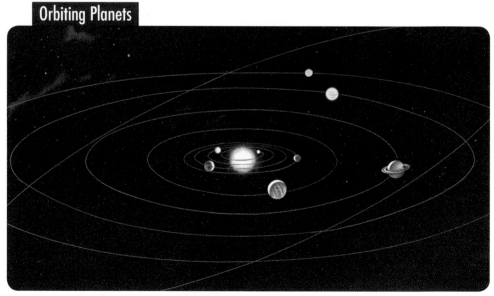

The planets orbit, or travel around, the Sun.

The Moon's Orbit

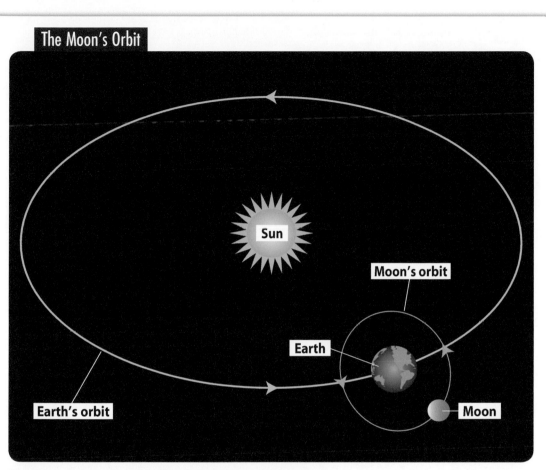

The Moon is a satellite. Satellites orbit, or travel around, planets.
The Moon is Earth's satellite.

Comparative Size of Planets

Sunny and Moonshine

Her name was Moonshine.
She was small and pale,
but her smile lit up the night.

Moonshine lived with Earth Mother.
They were very close.

Pluto

Jupiter

Uranus

Mars

Neptune

Saturn

Sunny and the Planets

His name was Sunny.
He was a famous star.
He put on a show in
the Sky Dome every day.

One evening, Moonshine saw Sunny's show. "I have to meet him!" she declared.

"You will have to get around me first," said Earth Mother. "Why?" asked Moonshine.

"Look at him!" said Earth Mother.
"You two are night and day—
complete opposites!"

"Oh, Mother!" Moonshine cried. "He makes me glow!"
"I can see that," said Earth Mother.

For many weeks, Moonshine went to Sunny's shows.

Each time she arrived earlier. Each
time she got closer, but Earth Mother
always stood in the way.

"Please, Earth Mother!" she begged. "I'm so close!"

"Okay!" said Earth Mother. "Okay! Okay!"

Moonshine ran onto the stage.

She gave Sunny a kiss, and all the lights blew out!

"What is your name?" Sunny asked.

"Moonshine," she answered.

18

Sunny began to sing,
"I've been kissed by Moonshine. Now my heart is no longer in the dark."

The song became a big hit.

Sunny and Moonshine went together for a while. Then they began to drift apart.

Earth Mother was right. They really were night and day.

Once in a while, though,
they meet again and kiss
sweetly in the dark.

The End

A Solar Eclipse

Total Solar Eclipse

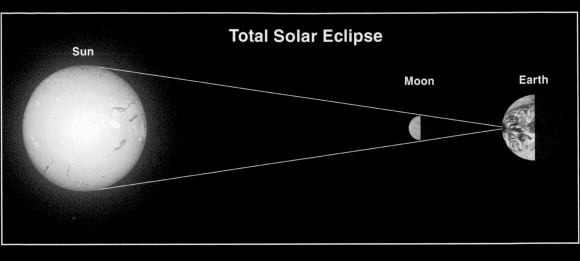

Sun

Moon

Earth

Total eclipse as seen from Earth

Once every few years, the Moon passes between the Sun and the Earth. The Moon blocks the Sun's light, and the sky turns dark somewhere on Earth.